NAKED

POEMS

DONNELLE MCGEE

ISBN 978-1-936373-43-7

Cover art: © 2014 Donnelle McGee
Author photo: © 2014 Leslie Moore
Published in the United States by Unbound Content, LLC, Englewood, NJ.

The poems in this collection are all original and previously unpublished with the exception of those listed in the credits page at the end of the volume.

NAKED

First edition 2015

for Thera Denise McGee and Ron Levy,

thank you for life

What matters most is
how well you
walk through the
fire.

—Charles Bukowski

Table of Contents

I

Digging up Them Dreams 15
Inner City Blues 17
Muh 20
From the Fire 21
Riding the RTD Bus Down Crenshaw 22
Duracell 24
Blue Dumpster 25
The First Time I Spoke to My Dad 26
Room 212 27
Messin' With a Prostitute 28
How in the Fuck Did I Get Here 30
Don't Look at My Arms 32
What the Fuck Was I Thinking 34
On the Turn 35
Amber Shed Tears on Smoggy Blue Nights 36
In the Back Bathroom 37
Jimi, O Jimi, O Jimi 38
Long Before the Bullet Burned into His Head 39
Van Gogh Scares the Shit Out of Me 40
And Here I Sit 42
Hey Black / Jew Boy ... Welcome to Folsom Half-Breed ... 44
Cinnamon Man 47
Naked 48
Rewind 2 Gay 49
Stutter 50
Clifton 51

II

Love Turned Around 55
Dear Muh 56
Love Turned Backwards 58
In a Chevy Blazer in the Alley on 13th Ave 60
Once Had a Brief Conversation at a Strip Club in Arizona ... 61

I Could Fall Into Coltrane's Horn 62

Monsters 63

Homecoming 64

To the Kids Shot out of Cannons 69

Poem on Fire 70

Whiffs of Utopia 72

I Ain't Never 74

For Sekou Sundiata 75

Cut Me Open 76

Teeth Damned 78

I Love This Song 80

Sonia 81

III

Body Gone 85

Threesome 86

Lou Reed Is Singing Take a Walk on the Wild Side 89

My Heels Are Burning 90

Overheard at a Motel off Highway 99 92

10 — Ten Years Back 93

Knight 94

Sometimes I Wonder What My Mother Says at Her Meetings 95

Her Back to Me 96

My Jewish Grandmother 97

Leaving Her Body 98

Falling Awake 99

Paying for Flesh 100

I Ain't Movin' 101

Forget Me Not 102

Open Blues 104

But I Don't 105

Don't Know 106

Green Hills in Vermont 107

Dinosaurs 108

Home 109

She Has Her Lions Now 110

About the Author 113

Publication Credits 115

Acknowledgments 119

I

And I sat out my childhood with stutters and poems gathered in my head like some winter storm. And the poems erased the stutters and pain. And the words loved me and I loved them in return.

—Sonia Sanchez

NAKED

Digging up Them Dreams
13th Ave, 1978

We stand leaning on the steel rails bolted down into the porch, watching
The smog sap the dreary blueness out of the early evening sky.
Cousins Day-Day, Reese, El, and my little brother Ed and I
Hold our glare on what is to come. We hold shiny dimes and quarters in
the pockets of Our patched Tough Skins. Just back from a party run to
        Tanners Market for fire sticks,
Now-n-laters, lemon heads, grape crush soda, chips, Boston Baked Beans
and the likes. Months later I caught a mouthful of decay fuckin' with
Tanners. From El's porch we Look down onto Adams Boulevard and smell
        hot pastrami being done
Right at Johnny's. When the sun shrivels into the Pacific, some twenty or so
miles away from us, we catch the whiteness of the street lights bouncing off
the black tar of 13th Ave.

I remember us kids knee deep in green dreams: Reese
Was going to be the next coming of Dr. J.
Half the week I was Lynn Swann, during the other half I was Master G of
the Sugar Hill Gang, even though I couldn't rap like Day-Day and Ed.
Them two were going to
Be the rappers. El had dreams too
But I never knew his.

We sit on the porch for hours *cappin'* on each other.
Reese looking at Day-Day, telling us ...
This boy's head is so big he can barely keep his balance.
Then Reese, turning his eyes on me,
Saying ... *and look at your big ass teeth, big ass choppers. Chop. Chop.*
Damn teeth lookin' like a chipmunk's grill. And El, fat boy, don't move too much;
Your fat ass might bring this porch down.

Sometimes we fight and cry when the shit gets too real,
Only to be back on the porch in the morning talkin' about what we are
    going to do
With our lives.

And them dreams keep us going.
Until life runs up in your ass / buckles hope,
Ambitions halted at crooked angles.

And Day-Day graduated high school and enlisted in the Air Force.
And Reese became a Crip.
And El faithfully delivers the mail.
And Ed takes a bullet in the head.
And I turned inward.
And I wrote.

Inner City Blues
after Marvin Gaye

this is what i saw ...

mexican boy fall against
a chain
link fence   his jaw busted for five
dollars
and the crip say   *told you i was gonna take that fool's money*

saw this ...

mother in public put a belt on
her three year old

little boy taking a beating

mother swinging wildly at demons   little boy scarred
already

and this too ...

mi pops pulling mi hermano
off the top
bunk
and another belt high
up on a little boy's tender
back

this is what i heard ...

DONNELLE MCGEE

two young bruthas on the RTD   something like

nigga nigga nigga nigga nigga nigga nigga

and i thought we had evolved

and i remember ...

that same crip
flinging a paper plate filled with gram's best out the
buick
mac-n-cheese
cranberry sauce   turkey   yams and buttered rolls soaring over Crenshaw

and me thinking   *what the fuck is wrong with you?*
but them words never left my body

and i remember ...

my friend michelle taking a bullet in the
chest
but then
again   she couldn't wait to live on the wild side

and yeah ...

there she was   muh   telling her two young boys
i'll be right back ... heading to the store ... you want something?
i kept my hands in my pockets
yeah   *you*   but i never said that either

what marvin say ... *make me wanna holler ... throw up both my hands*

NAKED

and you learn to navigate an inner city landscape
all the while doing your best to keep the
head high
even when
you
want to
holler

Muh

there is beauty
in your rough-edged smile
and when your words rise above the stench of fresh manure
spreading across the *Central Valley of Cali*
i hold onto them
when i find
myself aimlessly cruising

for day old, cheap perfume whiffs of women
to soothe bumps and bruises

then i frown and regret that i never
got enough of you
before smiling
knowing how you sold

your body to men
like me
and from that
i came

when you could have easily
ran from me
you were brave
and allowed me to taste this world
and it doesn't matter
that i have spent much of my life
searching for you in beaten down motels
on the bellies of women
doing their best to survive

From the Fire
(for Seven)

i come from them smoggy
nights in LA
i come from the meeting of john and prostitute

i come from
the ohio players
shouting fire

i come from being
told   here   take these food stamps to the market and
      get some
milk for you and your brother

i come from under the sound of
copters   spotlights
in my living room   and bullets piercing temples
      nightly

Riding the RTD Bus Down Crenshaw

muh is mixing the white flaky carnation powder with cold tap water
here use this for you and your brother's cereal

i refuse it
imitation milk is not natural

muh stops to get ed a red jelly filled donut
i get the glazed

then she shuffles us onto the rtd bus
we savor the taste of the donuts

but really we are just happy to be with her
and it doesn't matter

that the fbi is lurkin'
and it doesn't matter

that we are nearly broke
and it doesn't matter

that muh carries the beat downs / scars from men on her body
and it doesn't matter

that people look at her and wonder
who is this little white boy holding her hand

before she buckles their stares with
yeah this is my son

then looking at ed and me and telling us
people are just so damn ignorant sometimes

NAKED

the next morning i try the carnation milk
it taste like vomit

and i learn early on
to endure

Duracell

Them muggy / smoggy mornings
We licked silver tips of 9 volt batteries

The sting / snap / zing
Making us come alive

As did games of cats and dogs
We on bony knees crawling the shag carpet

Waiting to be caught
Anticipating touch

Skin on skin
A rub

Hard poke
A thrust from behind

Pausing the absence of a disappearing mother
And a quickly passing childhood

Blue Dumpster

This scar of a star above my right eye
Reminds me of how easily blood
Escapes skin to meet air
And how you and I
Had to become steel

You and I wrapping our legs together in the bathtub
You and I letting our chest nipples meet
And the metallic taste of your lips absorbing
Red memories eaten by the hood

And behind this scar we are caressing each other
Bodies warming the coolness drifting below a savory joint
Homeboys locked in excitement
For the touch of flesh melts even the hunger for a mother and a father

The First Time I Spoke to My Dad

he asked me if my mom was a prostitute.

The rest went something like this—

She may have been.

Well, I knew a lot of prostitutes when I was younger. A lot of my friends were prostitutes.

After I hung the phone up, I sat on the couch thinking —

I know a lot of prostitutes too, but they ain't my friends.

Room 212

stairs leading to her
green eyes   pushed   away

watching rain, balmy / slick
slide down a streaked window

no hot honey just cold cream jelly
rubbed between diamond lips

ready to set off
ooohhhs and ahhhhs of paying folk

and under a stained
faded comforter

i enter moist flesh
as she drifts away

Messin' With a Prostitute

Son's Voice	*Muh's Voice*
	where are you at son?
two in the morning	
	why son?
pulling into another motel	
it doesn't matter	what?
	what?
that a woman was murdered	
	leave
here the other night	
	leave
park between two faded white lines	
	i'm not there
watch the girl peek from behind the curtain	
	she is not me
her pink palm waving me in	
	why son?
i have walked into rooms like these before	
	i see
i have walked in then right out of these rooms too	
	why son?
but tonight i enter to stay	
	i see
inside there is a bed and a tv on	
	this here is a business son
the girl's cell phone is plugged in	
	leave baby
resting on a nightstand	

NAKED

she asks me what i want to do

i just want to touch flesh

i just want flesh

sam cooke died
at a cheap motel

messin' with a
prostitute

mmmmmhhhhhhhummmmmmmm

How in the Fuck Did I Get Here

Met her on Live Links.

Let's meet.

Drive to a beat up motel called the Apex. I got the hookup. What is wrong with me? Before I arrive, she calls my cell. Asks me to pick up a lighter, condoms, and some lotion.

And here I am. This room. TV on. Queen size bed. Comforter pulled back.

And here she is. On the bed. Red G-string rising from her sagging jeans. She is high. She is not attractive. I am paying for this. I can't do this.

You don't tweak?

Naw.

You do anything.

Naw. Seen what it does to folks.

It makes me feel good, you know? I get amped up, like
   wheeeeeeeeeeeeeeeeeeee!

Knock on door.

Oh, that's my friend. I'm just going to buy a hit.

NAKED

This man. Dealer. Mulatto. Python tattoo across his neck. I don't want to glance his way too long. He looks at me. Long stare. What the fuck am I doing here?

She asks me if I mine if she does a line. What the fuck am I suppose to say?

Powder up her nose. A hit from the pipe. Smoke rising. Her brown face still. Her eyes rolling back and up. She holds the pipe towards me.

You wanna a hit? It makes sex so good. Makes me horny.

Naw.

She tweakin'. The man asks for a ride.

I just need a ride down the street. Won't take but a minute.

Naw. I can't. Sorry. I'm leaving.

He could take me out if he wanted. But for some reason I feel he won't.

You can't give me ride dude? Just down the street. Look, if I was going to jack you, I would have done it already. Just give me a ride down the street.

Naw, I gotta get home. My kids. I gotta get home.

The prostitute says don't leave. Stay. Why are you leaving? You don't have to give him a ride.

I look at her. She gone. Ready to be fucked. But I can't do it. I won't. I gotta get the fuck out of here before I crack.

Don't Look at My Arms

i sneak glances anyway
because i want to understand
the crisscross needle marks
resting on your cocoa butter flesh

i need to know
what kind of pain you ran from
back in the day because i feel it

in my stomach too
boxing me in
and i can only find release
on top of women

who just pocketed my money
that was pulled
from a joint checking account

i am here to hear about
your journey from
nebraska to oakland
and on to pocoima

tell me muh
let me know

did you smile often
as a little girl?

when was the first time
your body was taken from you?

NAKED

what went through your veins
when ed and i were
taken from you
on that blue-skied morning?

DONNELLE MCGEE

What the Fuck Was I Thinking

use to
exit
highway 99
fade
right
quick park
and
have this
frizzled meth head
shake
my dick
while i
sat
on her
lap

On the Turn

looking at her legs

she could be   28   29   30

but
on the turn

she shows her face

teeth smashed
chipped and missing

skin ragged

scabs red
opened from scratching

her face dying

like me out here
cruising towards death

DONNELLE MCGEE

Amber Shed Tears on Smoggy Blue Nights

I will forget when I slept in the queen-size bed and kept still
afraid to use my voice to save my brother

the rustling of the sheets

his lips
down low on our cousin

Close lids
Let that go

In the Back Bathroom

muh's *'holic* breath
is hot on my face
and here comes another goddamn sermon of how much I am loved

a body can take so much
but what does the boy do with what he saw?

i do not forget how black leather welts skin
i do not forget how a beating

    when it is done
    over
    and over

breaks my brother's spirit

and

i do not forget how her body twitched nose deep in caine
i do not forget her trips into the back bathroom to soothe the ache
i do not forget any of this
when i watch the mold wash away from the rock

Jimi, O Jimi, O Jimi

Jimi's guitar speaks,
crying, then fire-spraying
that good stuff on us.

Jimi, O Jimi,
O Jimi, Jimi, O O
Jimi, O Jimi.

And somewhere Jimi,
high, mostly on love and in a small lighted room—Holiday singin' /
    Coltrane blowin', leaves
his body again.

Jimi, O Jimi,
O Jimi, Jimi, O O
Jimi, O Jimi.

I hear it, the train
howling, you falling fast from
a purple red sky.

NAKED

Long Before the Bullet Burned Into His Head
Awake, 1987

I watch my brother vibe in our room Rakim's poetic voice
leaving the speakers of the boom box sitting on our dresser

This is a good moment I will leave for college in the morning and I wonder
about his fate In this house we sleep on foam beds Funds be too tight

In this house we can feel the
discolored walls I get to leave

So I watch my brother from a same mom
and a different dad

lose himself in the head of prince rapper Rakim My brother
damn near shouting

I start to think and then I sink
Into the paper like I was ink
When I'm writing, I'm trapped in between the lines,
I escape when I finish the rhyme ...

His crown the color of shiny copper A king with a spiral notebook full of
 lyrics
A rapper in the making And for the first time I realize leaving is easy

I understand the importance of Rakim I understand how my brother
finds himself How he will survive

Van Gogh Scares the Shit Out of Me

blinking silhouette
splashed with hot lights seduces the runway

letting her nakedness
intoxicate the sick

her slender arched feet
give me the blues

inside this strip club
along sunset boulevard

where Van Gogh's ghost
is hunched over my trembling back

and we lonely married men
yearn for young ripe flesh

while tupac's california dreamin'
booms above our heads

and the image of Van Gogh's print hanging on my daughter's wall
blinks in front of my eyes

as the girl dances like the wild cypresses
swaying above yellow wheat fields

swirls of blue and white colliding
on the end of Van Gogh's brush

before she climbs the gold pole
i smell the meat of her white thighs go snug, like a vice, around the coolness

NAKED

of the pole

i reach in my pocket for *mo-green*
keep feeding her crisp dollars because she is the free cypress

she the knife
grazing my neck

DONNELLE MCGEE

And Here I Sit

with the friction of the past
crashing in too quickly

and here i sit
as a white man

and here i sit
as a black man

and here i sit
on a motel bed wanting to ask this brown haired girl

how did she end up in a room like this
but i don't because she may ask me the same

instead she keeps one leg in her jeans
slips a condom on me

makes her vagina tight by sticking three fingers inside
and with her eyes closed she moves

and this is where i lose myself
a blend of two

right here right here
in this poem

roaming
between two worlds

blowing away from my blackness
trying to make right of my whiteness

NAKED

blowing away from my whiteness
trying to make right of my blackness

Hey Black / Jew Boy ... Welcome to Folsom Half-Breed

I. 1969
Black boy covered in white and stars atop the green cypress on a cool
February in Monterey Born between thighs of cocoa butter to be
questioned by Gram ...

Why is this baby so pale

Granddad say ...

He's for keeps though

Muh locks her eyes
thinks quick thinks white
knows me not to be Ivan's baby
Ivan is dead
young black man pierced by LAPD bullets as a bank robbery turned red

II. 1982

A white boy on the yellow Folsom School District bus is talking about how
his confederate uncle taught his two year old brother to say (   )

White boy say ...

He just repeats whatever you say and he said (   )

I the Black / Jew boy two seats back hold my eyes on my chest
not a Black face anywhere
so I turn to gaze out the window
silly shit like this floods my days in Folsom

NAKED

III. 1983

Boys my age enjoy the board game Risk
Eric, Joey and I pick our pieces

Joey say ...

I don't want the black pieces
I don't want the (   ) pieces

Tired of hearing it
my right hand meets the pink flesh of Joey
Eric understands

IV. I remember

my Uncle Roy
death close on him
rise straight up in his bed and ask ...

What do you want with me   Where do I go   *Where do I belong*

When I was deep in the muck of white Folsom
turned inward
to ask the same

What do you want with me   Where do I go   *Where do I belong*

But I could only scream behind closed lips
sitting on the toilet
legs flexed / crisscrossed
brown eyes wide open
as I released the sticky whiteness from my shaft

thinking how easier it would be
to be just white / just black

V. 1990

Black / Jew boy
tangled in two realms
a mixed nut would be too easy of a title to hold me under the table
and I didn't know my father was Jewish / Alive until Muh cut the truth
    open
ripping the fiber away from walls
to reveal Ron Levy

thank you   *Muh*
thank you   *Muh*
thank you   *Muh*

the crumbling complete

Cinnamon Man

In my gut
below my
heart is where I hear granddad telling me to put on Leadbelly
'cause the blues are now creaking

swaying

under our people's
soles.

And I wonder if granddad's ghost still wakes late
to grasp some solace from Cash and King.

The baritone voice of Johnny and the buzz

flying off

B.B.'s guitar
looping the record player, needle riding vinyl
as I peek into the black living room
to see this beautiful cinnamon man singing the blues,
rubbing them bruises
    away.

Naked

i am crying
muh is crying
sade singing
in front of us

i will find you darling and
i'll bring you home

when i stop
crying
my body is above me
watching over my body
and only a body can call its body home

Rewind 2 Gay

my feminine side need take it slow this lifetime

like this silver airplane above me now
hovering above the storm
waiting for a land signal
before it comes
black wheels slicing through pink and yellow petals
making its way onto a straight path
a runway to leave from and return to

and too i runaway
suffocate what burns under tongue
unspoken yet known 'cause it numbs
when i shoulder-stare him

keep it in
ice-water can erase these dreams
keep it real

wrap my legs around her
hide up in her
linger
flex
retreat

my feminine side need not wake this lifetime

Stutter

Slow down boy, you're biting your words.

Clifton

Slow me down

guide me in   guide me in

II

There is this edge where shadows
and bones of some of us walk
                    backwards.
                        —Joy Harjo

Love Turned Around

It's late
and there you are.

The buzz still jumping behind your cocoa butter flesh
blood speed through your weary body

you telling me
Donny ... Donny baby, honey, Gram loves you.

I'm awkward facing this blunt of affection
but I believe you

as the loops of our addictions find us both.
And the maroon daylilies in your front yard are wilting,

yet cancer is eating you up and down
and love slices pride

when I hear you are leaving the living.
So if I may, for today,

turn my love around to face you, knowing generations have the tenacity to store
one affliction for another,

numbness housed deep in flesh,
pressed and wet, and Gram, if only I had the strength,

I would eat that numbing away so quick
you'd think you were born again.

Dear Muh,
Dreaming, 1979

I saw you
your red heels slicing night
on the Ave. next to Johnny's pastrami stand

I saw you
struttin' over slick pavement
your white dress faded
threads running down its side

and you soared under the street lights
rising above Crenshaw
them beams got you on spotlight Muh
your arms held high and open
as if you were waiting for some knight to swoop you up

help you flow to a time
where you sat innocent in front of a television chewing on buttered
    popcorn
all the while giggling
your tight ponytail at rest between your shoulder blades

but this image fades
my dream cuts back to night
where you are sprawled out on some dirty motel bed
a drug dealer's prize

Muh
I saw you walking the Ave.
tell me I'm dreaming

NAKED

wake me
      won't you

           wake me

Love Turned Backwards

I haven't been in Gram's house going on three years now
hard to get home sometimes Keep out of them rooms

where the heater
melts cubes of butter

dull knife resting at their sunken sides the
night my grandmother scared the shit out of my cousin Warren and me

when she raced through the kitchen a gust not seen but felt
We hunkered together on the pull out bed in the den We couldn't see her

snap along the tile floor granddad put down on his hands and knees
for her

Still
we smelled JB on her breath and caught her deep eyes above us

and I ain't going back to that house
to flex naked at two in the morning flanked by mirrored living
        room walls To

release distant affection for a woman I never felt comfortable with
Tension sliced and wedged between us

When will she break me down Tell me what she really
wants to tell me Flush me with

Why'd you marry a Mexican
You think you too good for this family

NAKED

Why couldn't you just let things go Like finding your father
what, black ain't good enough for you Or are these my pictures

bouncing off this beautiful woman Me to her
digging up what I choke down in my belly

You ask me *are you nervous*
Let me scream in and along the curves of your ears Yes

Gram, I am always drying my pink palms around you
The edges of your personality cut me long ago

Your house be but a time in my chest Beats and beats of sweat
collected during them early years
nestled beside you Love turned backwards
figuring out how to hold off the crazy boiling in my head

without losing myself in the blues
of your home

Them frenzied vibes ricocheting over
my bowed head Gold bullet

still lodged in the skull of my brother laid
sprawled on the black street at the feet of this house

In a Chevy Blazer in the Alley on 13th Ave

I saw my mother take a blow, a brown fist meeting the meat-flesh of her left
    temple.
I watched her eyes go behind themselves as her head broke glass. And then a
second strike, a third thrust, a Boom Boom. What could I do but turn away,
sink back into the blue bucket seat and cradle my knees.

Once Had a Brief Conversation at a Strip Club in Arizona

the stripper: hey sweetie, you want a lap dance?

me: i'm waiting for her

the stripper: who?

me: her, up on stage. i'm in love with her.

the stripper: okay. don't know if you want to fall in love with a stripper, though.

me: yeah i know ... i'm just playin'.

the stripper: you sure about that?

me: actually i'm really in love with someone who looks like her.

the stripper: oh, well when she's done make sure you get a lap dance.

me: yeah, i'm gonna need a couple of 'em.

I Could Fall Into Coltrane's Horn

Lick scars on a body
Left to fend off the pimp's cold blue glare
And his right hand

A body told
Get your ass out there tonight bitch and don't come back until
       You got my muthafuckin' money

Hmm ...
Say I could fall into Coltrane's horn

Rescue a body before
It cracks to meth

Caress a body smooth
My tongue holding teeth in place before the falling out

Yeah ...
Say I could fall into Coltrane's horn

Descend with a body
Into a shiny gold opening

Monsters

There are no easy poems.
Red itch, first fury—
We poets cut muck out of our bodies,
Dicing layers Break us
together.

—after reading Sylvia Plath's "Finisterre"

Homecoming
Dreamy, 1981

I roll over onto my side and the heat coming from her exposed vagina, a couple of feet away from me, plugs my ears. Am I dreaming up in here?

Not sure.

I don't think I am though.

There we are. My brother, my cousin, Muh and I down for a nap atop the thick king-size mattress in the back bedroom. I wake to her most organic place being fondled, played with, and maybe even just vacated. Its black fuzz cover is pulled to the left.
My cousin's fingers in full exploration. His grin exposes the hugeness of his two crisp, white front teeth.

I am twelve.

My brother, three years younger than me, sleeps in the middle of the bed. His left shoulder slightly touches the bare shoulder of our Mother. He will sleep through the quiet ruckus of this overcast summer afternoon.

I am awake.

I hear the murmur of the color television. ESPN programming in its early existence brightens the small glass screen. I see the world's strongest men raise large logs over their square heads and fling them. They grunt. They release.

I move my eyes to my cousin.

He is two years older than me. He is already a Crip. His summer job, which he is good at, is to transport the unchecked heroin from his hometown of

NAKED

Los Angeles up here to Washington. He told me last week that the Continental Airlines flight into Seattle was too cool. I thought of those sweet plastic wings the pretty white lady in tan nylons gave me when I flew in.

Now he is a blur to me. I see a faint smile. His big teeth rest on his bottom lip. I see him pull his right hand away from Muh's vagina.

What does a kid do in a moment like this?

This room is getting smaller and smaller.
The fumes choking me. Her vagina. His hand. It's all in slow motion now.
I want to breathe.
I want the sun to burst free of the clouds and light this room up for all to
    see.

He sits on his knees situated inside the V shape made by the parting of
    Muh's legs.

My cousin looks like the mulatto kid, the one everyone calls Lost, I saw back in Los Angeles during the school year that was caught stealing from RayRay's Liquor Store. Lost was caught. He told me later he didn't care because the thrill of the moment, taking something that didn't belong to you, was worth it.

Muh is still sleep. But I hear her tell him to *stop playing now, shit.*
Her voice is so quiet I wonder if I really heard it.

I think about Frank. Frank is Muh's man. He is not a big man,
however, on the streets he is the *man*. Frank is the man who runs one of LA's biggest drug families. Sometimes we ride in his Chevy Blazer and he sings along with George Benson. Telling us boys ...
Give me the night, just give me the night. During this nap,
he is out of the apartment and at another apartment with another girlfriend.

65

DONNELLE MCGEE

Roses for all the pretty women is what he tells us boys.

In this here apartment, up here in this bed, what I'm seeing makes me want to wilt into the mattress. I make eye contact with my cousin, his amber eyes focus on me, but I know he is not seeing me. He pulls away from his aunt and sits at the front edge of the bed.
I sink back into the mattress. Brother and Muh sleep.

I listen for my cousin to make a sound.

I listen for Muh to wake.

I wait for clean whiffs of air.

I wait for the sun.

The fragrance leaving Muh's opened legs moves about the room. In my head I hear her vagina sing. Before I catch the melody of its rift I imagine how sound, its sound, can squirt out and find its way through the snugness of Muh's threshold. I lay on the bed thinking how the roughness and eagerness of two bodies tangled together can comfort and damn right heal. At least that's what it felt like when my cousin was on top of me.
I was younger then and we don't do that anymore.

But why did he have to enter Muh?

My body jerks. I use my hands to grab the pink top sheet. I hold its softness tightly in my damp palms. I let the sheet's coolness cover my face. Then the rhythm of Muh's vagina, its lyrical beat, warms me. I close my eyes and lay still.
I listen. I hear ...

NAKED

mmmmmhhhhhhhhummmmmmmm
it is ok
right here in this space it is ok my son
my son
my son
how we find ourselves in places where the sun cannot even penetrate into

a place where he
and he
and he
and he
and he

and he and ... he too ... cousin our blood he too
has gone into me for his own reasons
into me
as the ghost of his bloody father lurks close by him

see my son see
let your tight shoulders breathe because i have wings down here where flight originates

into me
they have entered to seek comfort from the shadows hammering on their souls
so i say to you

when you see a vagina up close again savor its luster
admire how it resembles the shape of love
respect its window
kiss it
love it as your homecoming

DONNELLE MCGEE

And then silence.

I am left with the soft footsteps of my cousin leaving the room.
I am left with the shallow breathing of my brother.
I am left with Muh. My weary / beautiful mother and her song.
I open my eyes to feel the sun creeping through the only window in the
　　room.

To the Kids Shot out of Cannons
Nightmare

I would not come here
Turn back
Turn back from the rugged road you come up
They've got cannons ready
Hot and stuffed with sawdust
Turn back damnit
There is no space
In this place for martyrs
First   steel cones are set at your feet
You will walk *no mas*
You will have no more metaphors to push onto the page
You have become the written crucifixion and this city will heat then fire
spray
Your bodies for all to see that war is here
Processed and ripe

Poem on Fire

Let this poem
shoot out of
my bare toes
twitching hands
and pointed fingers
let it race through
my open brown eyes
to find stillness
in chaos
lust in marriage
let it move down her bare body
and curl at the silver rings on her toes
to breathe some fuckin' Van Gogh into the deserts
dying for color
for some pizzazz
see this poem rise
with the crows
trumpeting before the feeding
that waits
feel this poem's tingling hickory
savor at its lips
the forgotten nectar
left on dance floors
in downtown clubs
see it
fire into the sky
scattering cries
into backyards of
hodiddydumdum suburbia
as it cums
all over us
with wildness

NAKED

just in time to unlock
cuffed wishes
watch it hop into friction
this poem is screaming
for the burning
feelings of expression
to flourish and barrel over
pent up anxieties of being
naked in the square

DONNELLE MCGEE

Whiffs of Utopia
Shit → Them Substances That Kept Us Sane

i didn't take the shit
the shit took me
raised up with the white-magic
me left to escape
shoot my own whiteness onto red sheets
i high as you muh on a seven day binge
and i waited for you to be you again

i didn't take the shit
the shit took me
muh's raised vein poked
on her way into the purple blaze
on hard tar streets with bright white lights set ablaze
under the deep black hood of night
where the shit made pop's whole body beat
and scared the shit out of me
when i watched his nostrils flare to applause the rush

i didn't touch the shit
the shit touched me
when you sat behind the wheel pops
me holding on not wanting to die
in the smoky cloud of *that good colombian shit*

how does a body smother them *jones* that called muh from
gram's house on thanksgiving day?
i got sick *jonesing* for her return

i never slept with the shit
but its aftershocks humped me
out there in the valley

NAKED

where you and pops played in the streets until dawn
then slept with the grave yard crew
and i don't blame
don't wish a change
because tribes find places to plant roots in all types of debris
a tribe embedded in shit that exudes
intoxicating whiffs of utopia
stark scents that tingle the spine

DONNELLE MCGEE

I Ain't Never
13ᵗʰ Ave, 1991

wanted to smoke crack

but today

the day that *blood* shot my brother in the head
bullet burning through his brown delicate flesh
spurts of red splashing onto the black tar of 13th Ave
my little *hermano* a pierced hummingbird cut off from motion
and muh racing down white cracked steps to see her youngest son halted

muh saying
they shot my baby ... they shot my baby ... oh jesus ... jesus ... they've shot my baby

and i say
i ain't never wanted to smoke crack

but today

a lip gushing spray of smoke up into my cranium
might just ease the jitters rushing through my ivory bones

NAKED

For Sekou Sundiata

Did your heart skip up
when you wrote the perfect line? Did the rhythm

of Malcolm's voice cradle / rock your own words? Were the streets of
Harlem calling you in? Was the time you spent writing your words down

a blue hibiscus wilting too quickly? When you went
under your poems what was there? Did your long-story get shorter?

When you went behind
your lines did you ever find that finished poem?

Sekou I never met you.
But I did hear your voice shake out them poetic lines that still flow
        throughout my body.

Oh Sekou

                you

                                                flew

                out of this world too fast,

you be them sun-beats bursting
off black streets.

Cut Me Open

Listen   Listen
cut an opening deep
in me / split my skin
crack my bones
relics of unrest
breaking / splintering
knee caps now shreds of ivory
elbows sliced away from limp forearms and soft biceps
one foot snapped / axed from an ankle
the other
turned upside down
to reveal
a sole beat down

cut me open

to see myself
                watching myself
                                climbing out of myself

attempting to rise up from this
slippery
deep
canal
impossible to vacate
still I do not drown

Not yet

and so i lug a backpack
full of poetry
sanchez, scafidi, saul, y neruda

NAKED

and watch how a head bleeds life
escaping home

but how does one rewind time
to let that bullet skip through air
a precise pierce into my body
where heat cuts my flesh
finding a place to inhabit
where i can feel
for there is where my death takes shape
and a bullet burns me a rebirth

Teeth Damned
after Sylvia Plath

lady asphalt walker
outside you be bad ass sassy
inside resides crunched redness
scars stacked softly on each
of your brittle rippled
white ribs

you keep that bad ass strut though
tipitty tat tat tat
cream heels cut night

nicked up body
them unseen dents
be breaking you apart though

sag of pears
no longer green
dangle for them cold hands
distant / unfamiliar
pink wet tongues
racing along your retracting flesh

bad ass beams
do more than see
they pierce
look past the hunger of johns
to where your belly rumbles

where you eat me up
puckered red lips
no longer holding back your white teeth

NAKED

stank taste
of this kill
in the air

DONNELLE MCGEE

I Love This Song
(for Reese)

The criminal dances in front of me.
He moves his chiseled torso,
Shuts his eyes and sings from his heart about the *Slide Show*,
And about the *Man Who Hurts So Bad*.
I stare.
I see his essence,
I see his full surrender.

NAKED

Sonia

when you signed *Shake Loose My Skin*
told me to keep writing brother
i did just that   no stutters on the page
just naked images
and ain't that the way to unravel it all
to let it fly from the body to
buckle knees softly
before standing knowing words save

III

I know the bottom, she says. I know it with my great tap root:
It is what you fear.
I do not fear it: I have been there.

—Sylvia Plath

Body Gone

This is how I can destroy myself.
    Like this—

Cruising dark streets,
Then naked driving deep into bodies heated with meth,
Blades not visible until later.

Threesome

She
like you   feels the layers of his loneliness

she
like you
peels it away
sits in it if need be   he needs you both

she knows his kind
adulterated rifts   on squeaking mattresses

you know his kind too
drunken mornings   forgotten drive home

so it is no surprise
when you meet him
each time he winces   she dies

each time you pour tea
each sip from cup

loneliness is like this   surrounded by talking
by lips
bodies jerking and going

NAKED

loneliness is like this
drunk to babble alone
loneliness is like this
two indian women
licking
each other's underarms
this is how loneliness tastes

drinking a heineken

peering at youtube

do you see him now?

loneliness is like this
white walls bare
he is only missing

asleep at four a.m. in a hot room

the straightjacket

loneliness is like you

far away

and like her

the girl across the way

loneliness is like this
bottle of tapatío
eating out calms
inside kills

a white refrigerator with only a

sleeping in the white room is
enough for him

DONNELLE MCGEE

but look in more

this man we all know
smiling for you
you are with him

not by choice yet

do you feel him calling?

you don't answer
you remain here

loneliness is like this
he will eat
a misguided bullet

listen

with him

like you like her

in this room

assigned in his head

no response needed

man waiting for nothing

if need be

she is here like you

in flames

Lou Reed Is Singing Take a Walk on the Wild Side

and then he was a she
but
she didn't tell
me
until we hit
them white sheets
at
motel 6

but
it
don't
matter

flesh
is
flesh

it
will hold

My Heels Are Burning

i let my body leave home to find home
breaking numbness away
cream skin pulling from bone
i fall to my knees

when the tears overtake me
and the white weeping birch kisses my bare toes
i shake my head in a frenzy to stop the crazy

then there is the pull of the prostitute (flesh)
waving me into the room
slipping of self into rivers of muck

sparks burning my heels
when i walk with fire past dirty motels
past broken bodies   *you want a date baby?* —
past women with missing teeth and open red scabs

have you ever watched your body leave itself and stare right back at you?

i let my soles move across bodies full of alcohol
jittery bodies high on blow
faces nose deep in white powder

i keep moving   i keep moving

heels digging in and out of them old stories
my cousin spooning me
my brother   me   my cousin
our three bodies rolling inside each others
my cousin
inside my mother

NAKED

inside me
inside my brother
me inside my brother
i need not question the reasons
these are known

Overheard at a Motel off Highway 99

the john:	how much for a hand-job?
the prostitute:	what you got?
the john:	forty
the prostitute:	can i see your dick?
the john:	what?
the prostitute:	can i see your dick?
the john:	i'll pass
the prostitute:	yeah, then good ... and take your ass home, son!

10 — Ten Years Back
(for Patrick Rosal)

thought i saw you
10 — ten years back
teen boy dressed in fatigues
your tagalog spirit not meshing
with the american flag stitched
onto the sleeve of your right arm

thought i saw you
10 — ten years back
awkwardly embracing
your baby bro and little sis
inside the united terminal
and there be no hugs for your tatay

thought i saw you
10 — ten years back
shaved head
brown flesh
weighted orange smile
your glum eyes humming through me

thought i saw you
10 — ten years back
eating the meat out of stale sunflower seeds
before you moved on
like them red leaves blowing
free from the stiff maple in your backyard

Knight

You don't know the full story
As these white boys got me second guessing
                              myself

Your black hands be like mammoth cinder boom blocks
Protecting my fragile inner-blackness from its whiteskinned shield
And the *lookeylous*
                    confused glare

Black man you tell them all
That's my son
While the other day i lowered my head under
The Windex streaked Chevy window for the school drop
                                                    off

And I wonder
Did you pick up on my shamefulness
Did your pride crumble like crackers smashed for the fry
As you watched me step out of the car and
over the pink lantanas
scraping the cracked cement

Hope you know now that I saw you as *mi lector*
I soaked in all your words *(Close mouth don't get Fed)*
Words that pummel in my soft chest still

                                        —*for Mi Pops*

Sometimes I Wonder What My Mother Says at Her Meetings

I see her rocking back and forth in a metal chair,
her tiny scarred hands held in prayer at her lips before she speaks.

What do you say Muh?

Maybe you say ...

*Hi, my name is Denise and I am an addict
and I've come out of the ash to reclaim my body.*

Maybe you say ...

*I'm tired.
My body can take no more.
And somebody tell my two boys I'm coming home.*

DONNELLE MCGEE

Her Back to Me
(for my grandmother, Johnnie Broughton)

from where i sit

      blades of ice loosen / drip slide
                    down a busted window

doctor has given her two days to two weeks

each   breath   now

terribly tender

no the morphine is not for you   but you may go closer   can you
    hear her heart
and when your blood overlaps / meets hers
be damn sure you too
will feel her leaving / buckle of the heart

                  a body run amuck

My Jewish Grandmother
If We Had Met
(for Victoria Levy)

I imagined walking into the nursing home,
whiffs of ginger ale and bengay
in the air, to see a brittle old woman.

I would watch her eyes move
from me to her son, and I would smile on her
holding back my tongue, silencing the words
of I'm your son's son.

And when she asked ...

Ron, Ronny, who have you brought with you tonight?

I would hold my breath,
close my eyes
and wait for my father to complete us.

Leaving Her Body

She tells me
with her soles
that the maple in our backyard cracked today,
its young trunk split in two —

She tells me
with her eyes
about the wind chime,
red-faced sun falling with the wind
shattering
red pieces resting on cement.

She tells me
with her lips
her love for what is lost
drags her heart down to poke at her ribs,

and just like that
a home is divided,

and just like that
I leave her body.

Falling Awake

No one tells you to leave. No one tells you to stay either; it's always something in between. Then again, you hear what you want. And there are moments when you find yourself lacing red Nikes for a long neglected run, putting clean socks away, or getting ready to pour wet pasta into the strainer, when your knees buckle. Thinking of how you got here. A new home. Kids half the week. And it's not that you dreaded being here, only you never imagined the stillness of this choice. An autumn leaf outside your window falling. Slowly. Time stopped, until the shiny, yellow leaf lands gently below and blows away.

Paying for Flesh

Our bodies retract,
and I leave her vagina
  wondering will this be the last time I enter these rooms looking for muh.

I Ain't Movin'

Thunder up on me movin' to a place where bricks stay down Thunder poundin' walls in on 13th ave Walls set ablaze I hear my train slammin' hard on the tracks of muh's cocoa butter arms Train a comin' fast My body now two One turned to look into the sun Me eyes lost The other holding the moon Belly full Hear my train a comin' Fire crackin' from my chest Rails rattlin' Them soles that stayed for the fear of fear now pressed deep in the earth Come on jimi Give me the train bra I want all the screeches Them sparks hoppin' up and down on steel Blues Reds I hear my train a comin' And i ain't movin'

— after "I Hear My Train A Comin" by Jimi Hendrix

Forget Me Not

If there can be
Two
Inside a body
Then let me speak to the
Other

                    Me. Red demon on your back.

Please, let me speak
To the
Other. You. I'm talking to
You.

                    I am you. Your guide to them streets.
                    Them dark, creped, lonely streets
                    Filled with black and red blazes
                    Of pussy for sale. 'Member Tijuana?
                    You want flesh. I take you to flesh.

Hear me. Because the day I
Left you
Pressed you out of me ...

                    But I'm still here. The lurker.
                    Red on your rotting, white bones.

You will not hold.
You will not hold. You will not.

                    Them rooms will. Them rooms we
                    Went. Smell of overworked pussy.

NAKED

Fresh semen shot into Trojans. When
Girls set up shop for the night. Boxes
Of Hostess donuts and Oreo cookies.
Cans of Rock Star. Nourishment for
Disappearing bodies once
Thighs parted.

Love will hold. I will write it down.
Then I will forget all of it.
I will forget you.

No. You won't.
You will never. Never. Forget me not.

DONNELLE MCGEE

Open Blues
(for Colleen Mills)

This is how it happens
when I let my body go. I let the numb hum away into
strange, used flesh.

This is how it happens
when I think what it would be like to be gay,
to once again know that touch.

This is how it happens
looking at my naked body in the mirror,
loving my sexuality to the point of release.

Only I know
Only I know
Only I know
Only I know

Like the wolf I am screaming at a white night.

And it happens,
I take my body back from these empty rooms; take my body back from
hundred dollar nights and a numb cum into a condom.

I take my body back
I take my body back
I take my body back
I take my body back

to the arc of its sexuality, to where my flesh waits for her,
that goddess,
to pinch my heart.

But I Don't

Middle-aged man blazed up on meth
Swinging a steel pole at a young woman
She defending herself with a green hula hoop
Pole missing this slender woman
No doubt she is hooked or nearly hooked

This is all a blur to me
In my car Santana's *Hold On*
Easing from speakers
As I zoom by
Wanting to   look back

Don't Know

much

spent
much
of my time here
chasing the hot
naked flesh of women

thought i'd find
some magical healing
leaving
their
fingertips

a touch i've yet to feel
probably
because
most of the time
i was paying them

don't know
much
but i do know
the sight of this
hummingbird
on the
maroon maple
in my backyard
is
damn near
spiritual

Green Hills in Vermont

This is how I can save myself
    Like this —

Listening to Cocker belt *With A Little Help From Me Friends.*

Reading Neruda.

Kissing the red and black medicine bag I keep tucked in my pant pocket.

Eating strawberries off her flat, white, pierced belly.

Visiting upstate New York, summer after summer ... after summer.

Running up and down them green hills in Vermont,
For here is where my third eye resides.

Looking at hummingbirds ... my kids making pancakes.

Dinosaurs
(for Wil)

My little boy is in the front yard digging up dinosaur fossils.
I watch him dig his silver hand-shovel into the black humus.

Look daddy, I found a dinosaur fossil.

Fossil: a record / recording of a time ago / a remnant / trace of an
organism

See, look daddy. It's a fossil!

He holds up a small grey rock. He is smiling. Our brown eyes meeting.
He is already stronger than I ever will be.

One day he will understand how a body has to return to the dark, wet earth.

One day he will hold this book in his hands and discover how organisms
mutate,
How his daddy excavated himself from the muck.

Home

the
soar of
winehouse
and
the succulent
groan
of simone
is
almost
as good
as
her
thin white legs
locked around
my arching
back

DONNELLE MCGEE

She Has Her Lions Now

I walk between the marble lions guarding muh's house
I pause at the end of her yard where green grass meets concrete
I glance back at lions
With their mouths open
With their teeth ready
And from the corner of my right eye
I see muh close the front door

About the Author

Donnelle McGee is the author of SHINE (Sibling Rivalry Press, 2012). He earned his MFA from Goddard College. He is a faculty member at Mission College in Santa Clara, California. His novel – GHOST MAN – is forthcoming from Sibling Rivalry Press. His work has been nominated for the Pushcart Prize. Donnelle lives in Sacramento and Turlock, California.

Publication Credits

Grateful acknowledgment is made to the editors of the following publications, in which some poems in this book first appeared, sometimes in different form:

"Dear Muh"	*Chaparral*
"Van Gogh Scares The Shit Out Of Me"	*Chaparral*
"I Love This Song"	*Open Cut (An Iodine Poetry Journal Summer Broadside)*
"Loved Turned Around"	*Pitkin Review*
"Her Back To Me"	*Quay*
"Knight"	*River Oak Review*
"I Ain't Never"	*The Dirty Napkin*
"Don't Look At My Arms"	*The Spoon River Poetry Review*
"Threesome"	*The Whiskey Island Review*
"Cinnamon Man"	*Holly Rose Review*
"Body Gone"	*Holly Rose Review*
"Green Hills In Vermont"	*Like One—Poems For Boston*
"What The Fuck Was I Thinking"	*Pale House*
"Lover Turned Backwards"	*RHINO*

"Falling Awake"   *SLAB*

"From The Fire"   *Two Hawks Quarterly*

"But I Don't"   *Umbrella Factory*

"I Could Fall Into Coltrane's   *Umbrella Factory*
Horn"

"Lou Reed Is Singing Take   *Umbrella Factory*
A Walk On The Wild Side"

"Riding The Bus Down   *Word Riot*
Crenshaw"

"Blue Dumpster"   *Word Riot*

"Once Had A Brief   *Word Riot*
Conversation At A Strip Club
In Arizona"

"Poem On Fire"   *Nomad's Choir*

Acknowledgments

Appreciation is given for the support, readings and suggestions from the following: Bhanu Kapil; Kenny Fries; Beatrix Gates, Louise Hammonds; Colleen Mills; Wendy Langford; Jonathan Brennan; Rigoberto González; Theresa Tran; Theresa Senato Edwards; Edward Leo Gills; and Patrick Rosal. And thank you too to El Monie and John Spencer for the beautiful photos and support of this book.

Thanks to Bryan Borland, Charles Rice-González, Bruce Guernsey, and Lee Herrick.

Special thanks to Annmarie Lockhart for making this book a reality.

And much love to Wil, Nia, and Leslie Moore.

Praise for NAKED:

"I watch my brother vibe in our room ... and I wonder about his fate," Donnelle McGee writes in "Long Before the Bullet Burned into his Head," and I am reminded of the pain and beauty of James Baldwin's "Sonny's Blues," and the quest of its nameless narrator to find his brother, too, lost in a haze of drugs and jazz. Through these poems "screaming/for the burning/feelings of expression," McGee's search in *Naked* is for his "muh" and father as well, and for his own sexual identity. Perhaps one day, as McGee writes in "Dinosaurs," his own son "will hold this book in his hands ... and discover ... How his daddy excavated himself from the muck." With these bare and searing poems, he surely has.

> —*Bruce Guernsey (former editor,* The Spoon River Poetry Review *and author of* From Rain: Poems, 1970-2010*)*

In these poems, Donnelle McGee has given us both a harrowing memoir of destruction and a slender talisman of salvation. You will be changed by reading this book. And if you have ever doubted the power of poetry to hold and bear the unbearable, to redeem what had appeared beyond redemption, *Naked* may just make you a believer. This is an astonishing book, excruciating, unflinching, lyrical and raw. It drew me in, broke me into pieces, and purified me in its fire.

> —*Ruth L. Schwartz, author of* Edgewater *(National Poetry Series 2002)*

These brave poems are road maps into (and out of) a difficult past, a landscape of drugs and bodies for sale, mothers and family swirled in despair. This is a hard ride not for the faint-hearted. Brace yourself. But keep your eye out for the nuanced beauty in the poet's hope. McGee fearlessly chronicles love, danger, and tension in a new style of confessional. This is a powerful first book of poems by a poet with a massive heart.

> —*Lee Herrick, author of* Gardening Secrets of the Dead

For Donnelle McGee, the stories stayed—days and nights of holding himself, fear pulled tight into his bones, then reaching for others, flesh to not forget, but remember home. He sees hard and close the changing motel of never enough and full acceptance, as the bullets of relieving addictions make their own path. In the crossfire, McGee, full of urgent and distant family voices, calls his body home to a tune of surrender. He tells all the stories and the repeating, naked. He wrote it down, he got it.

—*Beatrix Gates, author of* Dos

Praise for *Shine* (Sibling Rivalry Press 2012):

"Donnelle McGee's powerful, poetic prose gives *Shine* a unique voice that is fresh, bold and completely seductive. Like Rechy's *City of Night, Shine* brings us a hustler with a troubled soul, but sets itself apart with lush language that will echo in your memory and a lead character who will burrow his way into your heart."

—*Charles Rice-González, author of* Chulito

"Shine is tenderness incarnate. All the love, violence and need of a life-time happen in the time it takes to read this brilliant, brief and searing new book by Donnelle McGee. I was altered by the reading of it. Then I read it again."

—*Bhanu Kapil, author of* Incubation: a space for monsters
and Schizophrene

"Donnelle McGee finds the intersection of elegy, violence, and eros in Shine. His novella etches into language the longing, bewilderment, affection, and grief of lovers, family members, and strangers. Crafted in finely compressed narrative fragments, McGee's story details the kind of material and psychic anguish most American writers would rather not consider. McGee gazes into the most difficult material unflinchingly. His pacing and language will keep you hooked with astonishing understatement and compassion. For its sustained terror and love, Shine is an utterly singular debut."

—*Patrick Rosal, author of* My American Kundiman
and Uprock Headspin Scramble

Selected Titles Published by Unbound Content

All That Remains
By Brian Fanelli

Backwoods and Back Words
By Nicole Yurcaba

A Bank Robber's Bad Luck With His Ex-Girlfriend
By KJ Hannah Greenberg

Assumption
Earthmover
By Jim Davis

At Age Twenty
By Maxwell Baumbach

Before the Great Troubling
Our Locust Years
By Corey Mesler

Captured Moments
By Ellenelizabeth Cernek

Early Harvest
By Euphrates Arnaut Moss

Elegy
By Raphaela Willington

Garden
By Ellen Kline McLeod

In New Jersey
By Julie Ellinger Hunt

Inspiration 2 Smile
By Nate Spears

Just Married
By Stan Galloway

Memory Chose a Woman's Body
By Angela M Carter

Painting Czeslawa Kwoka: Honoring Children of the Holocaust
Paintings by Lori Steiner
Poems by Theresa Senato Edwards

The Pomegranate Papers
This is how honey runs
Wednesday
By Cassie Premo Steele

Riceland
By CL Bledsoe

Saltian
By Alice Shapiro

A Strange Frenzy
By Dom Gabrielli

Written All Over Your Face{book}
By PMPope